# ⬦ CONTENTS ⬦

# What Does *Alive* Mean?

Every single living being has a beginning, a time to be alive, and then an ending, or death.

During your lifetime, your body is busy doing its work. You breathe, move, eat, see, hear, touch, taste, smell, grow, talk, play, think, and feel. Yippee! You're alive and a part of the world.

5

# Why Does Someone Die?

Dying is a part of life for every living thing. Death happens for different reasons. Someone may die after a long illness, so everyone knew he or she was going to die.

Other times, it's a complete surprise.

Hurry! Hurry!

Emergency Room

A life can be very long or very short. Even someone just born may not be strong or healthy enough to stay alive.

6

Others may die from being hurt in an accident.
Even when doctors and nurses do everything possible to help,
some accident victims do not recover.

Sometimes lives are lost violently such as when someone kills someone else. It may be in a war…

or for reasons that are very hard to understand, such as poverty, prejudice, and drug abuse.

Someone may even be so upset and without hope about his problems that he kills himself. This is called suicide. All kinds of death make people sad.

Most of us live long, healthy lives. A child, a mother, or father usually lives until he or she is very old.

9

# What Does *Dead* Mean?

When someone dies, her body stops working. The heart stops beating, and breathing stops. The brain doesn't send or receive messages. She no longer can see, hear, touch, taste, smell, eat, play, feel, or think. She cannot move.

Someone dead may look asleep,
but she isn't sleeping and she
cannot wake up.

11

# Feelings about Death

When someone you care about dies, you may have all kinds of feelings. It may be hard to believe that a dead relative or friend won't be around anymore.

It's not true. Grandma isn't dead.

She is, too!

In my dream, Yoyo was still alive.

You may have a hard time getting to sleep or have strange dreams or nightmares for a while.

I dreamt a ghost was chasing me and I was running away.

Losing someone who is special to you is *very* hard to understand.

Please, God, let Daddy be alive again. I want him back.

13

You may feel so sad and lonely that it hurts. These feelings are not always easy to talk about, but it helps if you can.

It can be very scary when someone close to you dies. You might wonder about how your life will change.

**Can we keep our house?**

**Yes, we can. Try not to worry about that.**

You might worry whether you will die, too, or if someone else you love will die.

**Will I get sick and die like Cousin Boris?**

**A healthy kid like you? Not likely.**

Things you weren't afraid of before may scare you now.

**What if we crash, too?**

**Well... I will drive very slowly and be extra careful.**

It's also natural to feel angry when you miss someone so much. Some days you may push away the very hugs you need. There are lots of ways to let out mad feelings without getting in trouble.

You may want some time to yourself…

and time to be near those you love best.

Some things are worth crying about.

When someone you love dies there is no right or wrong way to feel.

17

# Among Friends

When someone in your family dies, your life is likely to be different. But you hope your friends will treat you the same way they did before.

18

Invite her over to play.

I don't want to talk about it.

It may be hard for your friends to know what to say or do to help you feel better.

This is a special time to show
your love and respect.

Friends and family will want to help you honor the life of your friend.

A funeral is a special ceremony for someone who has just died.

No more lettuce for Harriet.

Going to someone's funeral or memorial service is one way to let a family know you share some of their sadness…and some of their good memories, too.

Even if you don't go to the funeral, you can help out at home, offer extra hugs, or make up a special good-bye poem.

25

# Keeping Customs

There are many special ways of doing things that help us say good-bye to someone who has died.

Some families burn incense and bow low in front of the grave.

Others sing and pray together at the grave. Part of their circle is left open in honor of the dead one's spirit.

Still other families spend several days in mourning by sitting shivah. They sit on a simple wooden bench and light a candle every day.

Some families have the coffin buried underground. Others choose cremation.

Many families continue to honor the dead long after they have died. They may say prayers or prepare a special offering.

# What Comes after Death?

Some things about death and dying are very hard to understand, even for grown-ups. No one can know for sure what comes after death, but almost everyone has an opinion about it.

If you have questions about it, ask your family or your religious leader.

29

# Ways to Remember Someone

Even when someone you love dies, you don't lose him completely — you still have your memories. That person can always be a part of you. There are many, many things you can do to remember someone.

Make a scrapbook about her.

Play the game "I remember when..." with your family and friends.

Look at his photograph.

Keep practicing something he taught you.

Write a poem about her.

Keep something of hers in a special place.

Visit her grave.

At other times you may be busy having fun, making friends, learning something new. This is not forgetting the one you love; it just means you're doing other things. Hurray for life!

# GLOSSARY

**autopsy:** careful medical study of a dead body to find out exactly what caused death

**cemetery:** place for burying the dead; graveyard

**coffin:** box in which a dead body is buried or cremated

**corpse:** dead body, usually that of a human being

**cremation:** the burning to ashes of a dead body

**funeral:** service, often religious, held to honor the dead at the time of burial or cremation

**grave:** hole dug in the ground to hold a coffin, usually covered over and marked by a gravestone or other marker

**hearse:** a special car or other vehicle used to carry the coffin at a funeral

**memorial service:** service held at any time to honor and remember someone who has died

**mourn:** to feel or express sadness or grief for a death or other loss

**next of kin:** closest living relative

**wake:** a watch over a dead body before burial; a viewing

**widow:** wife of a person who has died

**widower:** husband of a person who has died

**will:** written directions for what is to become of someone's personal property after death